* * *

THE DEEP SEE

How to See into Your Soul and Find Who You Are and Want to Be

by Naomi Bareket

* * *

* * *

"85% of successful Executives who graduated of Harvard say that the key to their success is attitude. Your external results come primarily from your internal beliefs system and self-concept.

In this inspiring book, Naomi Bareket brings empowering insights and easy to apply tools to master a winning attitude, while aligning with your true self, and yield a personal and professional success."

-Brian Tracy, Author, Speaker, Consultant

* * *

THE DEEP SEE

Copyright © 2015 by **Naomi** Bareket

DEDICATION

Dedicated to my beloved brother Itiel Atzmon, of blessed memories.

* * *

SEE DEEP INTO YOUR SOUL AND FIND THE SEA OF POSSIBLITIES IN YOUR LIFE

I truly hope you enjoy THE DEEP SEE. Since the possibilities for applying these principles are endless, and the goal is for everyone to grow, progress, and fulfill his or her potential, let's continue our conversation. Here are some ways you can do this, and I look forward to hearing from you:

Facebook: Naomi Bareket
Business Facebook: neuroSUCCESSology
www.neuroSUCCESSology.com
neuro@neurosuccessology.com

ACKNOWLEDGMENTS

My many thanks to…

G-d who gives me strength and inspires me.

The many loving people in my life who surround.

My parents Ester and Haim Yosef Atzmon for raising me with so much devotion, love and joy.

Rami Bareket, my husband, who allows me to be who I am, always encourages me, and supports me with his love and wisdom.

My children Naama, Immanuel, and Itamar, who are so patient in my journey.

My editor Gini Graham Scott, who dedicated many hours to make sure my manuscript is ready.

The artist, Mishell Swartwout, who allowed me to use her drawing for this book and workshops.

The people who provided their insights on Facebook and in my workshops.

Chris Pareja and Lana Tran, who reviewed the manuscript.

George Wilson, for his friendship and support.

TABLE OF CONTENTS

INTRODUCTION

I recently pointed out on Facebook that pictures can be a powerful source of learning:

> "I was invited to give a lecture at a conference in New York. Among other things, I'm intending to use the following picture. No wonder Napoleon Bonaparte has reportedly said "a picture is worth a thousand words." There are so many things you can learn and teach from this photograph. What can you learn from this photograph?"

One of the images I have used to get clients and participants in my programs to think about themselves and consider who they are, want to be, and present themselves to others, is the one shown on this page. It's a picture in which the cat looks in the mirror and sees itself as a tiger. Using this image often helps people project their own perspectives onto the cat as it looks in the mirror, and they can imagine what they might see as they look into their own mirror. Plus, it can help them find their true selves, although one can use other images which similarly have a strong personal resonance.

How this Book Came to Life

This book was born after I saw this drawing of the cat and tiger at a craft show. I fell in love with it because it spoke to me; it touched my soul. So, I bought it.

I said to myself, "I can use this picture at the NLP trainings, inspirational lectures, workshops, and seminars that I give." So, I took it to my trainees and my women's empowerment group, and I was excited about the overwhelming results and impact it had on the attendees. I felt that I touched them on a much deeper level and inspired them, because I shared the image with them.

I was too excited to fall asleep that night, and I sensed that I must share my insights with the world.

So, I posted the picture on Facebook to get perspectives from others through crowdsourcing. People responded strongly and shared their thoughts about the picture on different groups on Facebook.

Seeing that it had such an effect on people, I said to myself: "That's it!!! I must share this amazing enlightenment." So, I'm writing this book to share the inspiration I received from my experience of how a single picture stimulated many people so deeply.

My original purpose for this book was to equip you, so you could gain the wisdom and motivation I did. As I was capturing all the inspirational points, I personally learned from this picture along with feedback from others about it, I realized that speakers, managers, or anyone who wants to touch other people's hearts can use this amazing technique, too.

The book has evolved to empower you with all the epiphanies I gained from a single picture, and to share how similar processes can help you deepen self-awareness in your own life and the lives of others.

May you learn to "see" deeply and recognize the possibilities open to you from looking at this picture or from other images that resonate strongly with you.

Who Will Find This Book Useful

This book is designed to help individuals who want a deeper insight into their real selves and unconscious minds. It will help you discover who you are, set goals, and get empowered and inspired. It combines breakthrough techniques using visualization, pictures, insights from neurolinguistics programming or NLP, and teachings from the Bible. It is based on using a visual image, along with self-talk and other sensory techniques, to help you find out who you are, want to be, and other personal insights. I have found the image of the cat looking at the tiger especially helpful in providing inspiration and affirmations which you can use in your personal development, though you can use other images that trigger a strong connection for you.

In addition, the book is a good guide for coaches, lecturers, speakers, managers, CEOs, and people who conduct workshops, since they can use pictures in their practice. Also, managers and CEOs will find using pictures an easier way to communicate a message to their employees as a group, as well as reach out to each employee on a more personal level. This approach is a way to give employees personal attention by helping them think about the meaning and value of their jobs, so they experience more satisfaction. It also contributes to better communication and rapport between employers and co-workers.

CHAPTER 1: AN EXERCISE FOR YOU: WHAT DO YOU SEE IN THE PICTURE

A picture is worth 1000 words. There is so much you can learn by just looking at a picture.

Take some time to just look at this picture. Gaze at it for 30 seconds to a minute and notice what thoughts, revelations, or images come to mind. Write them down, so you remember them, or say them into a recording device. Notice whatever impressions come to you – and don't try to think about them now. Let whatever comes to you do so without any kind of mental review or critique. That will come later. For now, leave your mind open to whatever comes into it, like a flowing river, and just notice what is there.

What do you see or learn from the picture?

Write down your observations from this picture. Write down any thoughts or images that come to you. Nothing is

right or wrong. Just write down whatever you think, see, feel
or experience.

_____

_____

_____

_____

_____

_____

Notice your present mood. How are you feeling right now?
Do you think what you saw in the picture has anything to do
with your mood? Describe your mood -- the way you are
feeling in the present moment.

_____

_____

_____

_____

_____

_____

How do you think what you saw in the picture might have influenced your present mood? If it didn't have an influence on you, note that, too.

_____

_____

_____

_____

_____

_____

_____

The image used in this exercise is a powerful one, which I have used for this book. Later, you can use this same exercise with other images that resonate with you.

Now that you have experienced this exercise with fresh eyes and a clear mind, without expectations, in the next section, I will discuss what you might expect to gain from looking at this or other images. I will also talk about what others have gained from looking at this image.

CHAPTER 2: UNDERSTANDING WHAT YOU HAVE SEEN

You got a chance to look at the picture and responded from your heart before you were influenced by what other people saw in the picture. We are constantly exposed to all sorts of influences, such as the input of our parents, family, and peers; the teachings from our school and congregation; the latest news presented by the media; and the latest comments from our friends on social media. Therefore, it is important to give ourselves time to meditate and to "think for ourselves," isolated from any outside input.

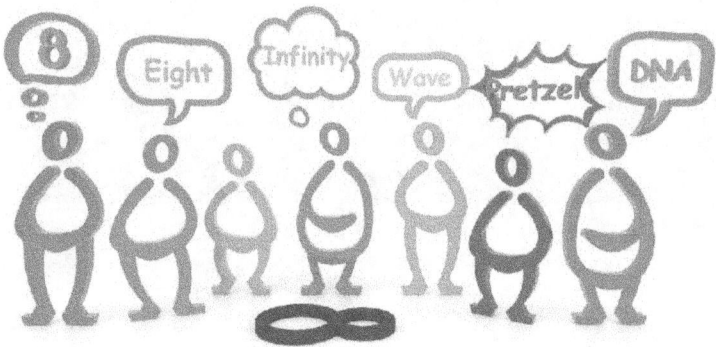

Why Do Different People See Different Things in the Same Image?

When I show the same picture to different people, why do I get different perspectives from different individuals?

In NLP, we say "The map is not the territory," which means that when one is presented with a map, other image, or reality, everyone sees what he or she wants to see, needs to see, or feels like seeing at a specific moment. That's because each individual is unique. Isn't that beautiful? We each have our own unique way of experiencing the world and interacting with others. It is the meaning and interpretation that you give to reality that makes you who you are.

We also see different things because we "edit" the information we see, so we aren't overwhelmed by the huge amount of input we receive daily. Otherwise, we would experience information overload. When we do this editing, we apply our own filters based on our past experiences and external influences. In the process, since we can perceive only a limited amount of information per second, we quickly delete, distort, or generalize some of the information.

Deletion occurs when we miss some of the information or leave out part of our experience.

Distortion occurs when we modify or exaggerate the accuracy of something or we assume certain things that are not true based on what we see. For example, we see a rope and think it is a snake.

Generalization occurs when we take a specific experience and think that it is one of a large number of experiences that are all the same. For example, if your little dog can't find his way back home, you generalize that all little dogs can't find their way back home.

We use these various filtering processes when we interpret things from the information we take in. Then, based on this processing, we form our own mental representation which determines our behavior, action, and reactions.

Therefore, what you see and how it makes you feel is very personal to you. Your perception is a reflection of who you are now, of your past, and of your wishes.

When you think about something, you will often see whatever you frequently think about. Commonly, you see what is relevant to you and things that relate to your current profession or studies. For example, when I was joking with my hair stylist and asked her if she readily noticed the cat's hair, she really did!

Thinking about something will also lead you to see it more frequently. Suppose you think about buying a specific car; all of a sudden you will see that car everywhere. Or suppose you learn a new word, and soon you hear it everywhere. There have been many times when I learned the meaning of a word in school, and then went home and watched a movie or read a book in which I noticed that the word was mentioned multiple times. This increased awareness occurs because when something is on your mind, you are more aware of it around you and notice it more.

Some Examples of Different Ways of Seeing the Same Image

To illustrate these differences in the way people see the same image, a few people at my seminar described their different perceptions of the expression of the tiger's eyes in the picture of the cat looking at the mirror. While some didn't even notice the tiger's eyes or expression, the participants who did see the eyes differed greatly in what they saw. Some described the eyes as kind or eager, whereas others characterized them as sad or happy -- two opposite extremes. What is amazing is the way one person can consider the same expression to be sad and another can think it is happy, showing how the same image can result in vast differences in what people see or interpret.

Different perceptions can occur when people look at you and think you are feeling one thing and other people think you are feeling something else. You might have one reading on a particular person and someone else might have a different perception. You each might see something different in the image at different times. You need to be careful to avoid coming to conclusions about what a person is thinking or feeling based on mind-reading someone else's facial expression or words. To know what a person really is thinking or feeling, rather than trying to read the person, just ask him what he thinks about something or how he feels. Ask yourself: when you looked at the image of the tiger, did YOU notice the eyes? There is no right or wrong answer. You see what you see based on the physical qualities of your eyes, your past and current experiences, and your current interests and focus.

When you looked at the image, what did you NOT see, based on learning what others saw in the image? As I found out when I asked this question in my workshop, some people didn't notice the eyes of the tiger, the colors, or other details. Conversely, some people noticed only the eyes. A benefit of doing this exercise in a group is that you can learn from what you <u>don't</u> see, as well. What you don't see is also affected by your personal preferences and your internal representation.

Looking Deeper Within

Now that you have looked at the image of the cat and tiger, without much conscious thought, you can learn how to look even deeper to learn more about yourself. While you can do some of this deeper looking on your own using this book as a guide, it helps to have a coach or teacher to guide you.

What's important is that different people see different things in the picture. While the picture actually shows a cat looking at the mirror and seeing the image of a tiger, some people see a lion, which feels good for them, and that's fine. A reason for this different perception is that the individual wants the image to have certain characteristics he or she associates with a particular image. In this case, the individual may see differently because he or she views the tiger as wily, clever, aggressive, and sneaky, whereas the lion is bold, strong, powerful, and regal -- qualities the person wants to acquire, rather than those associated with the tiger. So, seeing a lion in the mirror rather than a tiger is appropriate for that person, because it is what he or she wants to see.

Another difference is that some people relate what they see in the image to a past experience or to an even earlier experience as a child, while some people relate the image to what is happening now. Still other people may reverse who is doing the looking in the mirror, such as one man who imagined that the tiger was looking in the mirror and finding the kitten in itself, which he recognized as his way of looking at the little child within himself. Thus, he took the opposite perspective than usual, in that most people saw the cat looking in the mirror. Since he is a man in his 70s, the image made him feel young and joyful. Apparently, his memories from childhood were revived by this exercise, and he liked to access his childhood self as a source of positive energy.

He reached this realization as a result of us going into more depth about what he saw in the picture. This occurred in this way:

I asked him: "What do you see in this picture?"

He answered with the following statements:

"I see a tiger seeing the little kitten in itself."

"It reminds me that although I am old, often when I look at the mirror, I see the little child in me."

"It keeps me young in my spirit when I see the joyful child in me."

When you look at the associations and insights triggered by the image, it is important not to be judgmental or critical about your experience. Whatever you see in the picture is fully acceptable, and you should respect whatever you see for the insights you gain.

How Your Conscious Mind and External Influences Can Affect You

The purpose of looking deeper into your unconscious mind is because due to external influences, we often experience an inner identity conflict. These external influences suggest we should be one thing, while our true self tells us we really want to be something else. Is that true for you? Here are some questions to ask yourself:

- When you look at the mirror, do you see your deeper identity?

- Do you see only the surface and your impulsive reaction to things? Or do you also bring back the parts of yourself that are suppressed?

These external influences come from a number of sources. As growing children, we experience all kinds of feedback from our surroundings, and we build walls within ourselves or conflicted parts of our unconscious mind as defense or survival mechanisms. For example, if your parents forbade you from being silly when you were growing up, you had to hide this inner trait and suppress it. Whenever you have to repress a quality you want to express, that creates a gap between who you want to be and what other people expect you to be.

This experience from your childhood can carry over into your adulthood, even though you may not be aware of it. That's what happened to one client who told me that every time she visited her parents, she became very emotionally distant from her father. She feels that she was not her real self when she met with him, because she acted the way he expected her to act, not how she really wanted to be.

This conflict between who you are and how you feel you should act affects many people, and that disconnect can cause you to experience deep emotional stress. For instance, how many times have you told yourself: "I will not be hurt by what a certain person tells me," yet you keep letting that person hurt you? How many times have you told yourself: "I will not eat junk food," yet you eat that food, as if something stronger than you takes over your free will?

We often don't recognize ourselves due to this split between who we really are and who we become to please others. This split occurs since a baby's mind, which is like a *tabula rasa* or blank slate, receives impressions from others it comes into contact with, such as its parents and siblings. At the same time, the baby is born with certain propensities and personal traits that may or may not be congruent with these impressions. This lack of congruence is what leads to this split, which can become wider and wider as a child grows up.

The good news is that you can learn to access the true, inner you. One way to do this is through self-talk, which is often very therapeutic. You can personify parts of yourself and talk to them as if you were talking to a person, which can be anyone, from a friend to a guide, teacher, or angel. Some people even personify animal guides and teachers and gain insights from them. Like many people, you may find it easier to connect with who you really are by personifying the parts of yourself.

To bring balance into your life and become happier, you want to access the authentic you. A powerful way to do this is to have a dialogue with the different parts of yourself which you suppressed. Just as you can communicate with the parts of yourself that you already recognize, you can personify these suppressed parts which still exist within you but have become dormant. By communicating with them, you are in effect waking them up, so they play a more influential part of your life. You are bringing back to life the real you that is lying hidden within.

Let's say that you notice that you respond in an impulsive way, when someone has different opinion than you.

As a result, you may be insulting or put down that person because they don't see things as you do. Later, you are sorry about what you did. You realize you were out of line in creating a confrontation with someone just because they had a different point of view.

To change the way you react and, therefore, your behavior in the future, talk to the impulsive part of yourself. Imagine that part of you is a person you are speaking to and ask him what his higher intention is and what he wants instead. At the same time, you can bring up the part of yourself that is soft, accepting, and tolerant of others' opinion and talk to it, too, so you bring that part of yourself back to your life. By doing this, you empower the part of yourself you want to be.

I used this approach myself to deal with my own issues growing up as a child in a big family. Since I came from a big family, I wanted to make everybody around me happy, especially my parents. I still like to make everybody happy. At the same time, I wanted to give legitimacy to my feelings, desires, and wants, and overcome my tendency to put these parts of myself down. I wanted to reconnect with the suppressed part of myself and talk to it, too. When I did, I gave it more power and vitality, so I became more naturally aware of my own wants and needs and validated them. As a result, I now consider what I want and not just what makes other people happy.

A good illustration of a similar inner struggle and how these different parts of yourself can be in conflict is the struggle going on inside Riley's head in the movie *Inside Out* by Pixar. Riley tries to keep herself and her parents happy.

She goes through an inner struggle of emotions (fear, anger, disgust, sadness, and joy). The process is similar to the way you sometimes hear different voices in your head. When sadness takes over, Riley needs to find a way to access her joyful part, so she engages in a self-balancing act by using an inner dialog to overcome her automatic brain's interpretations of the situation. You can do the same by calling on the voices which represent different parts of yourself, which is a good way to sometimes manage your intense emotions.

Since we see more of something when we think about it, why not choose to think about good and positive things? Then, you will invite more good and positive things into your life. You will see them much more in your surroundings and have more positive experiences.

What you see affects your thoughts, too. Choose to see positive and inspiring things, and those will affect your thoughts and actions. You can also decide what you want to focus on at a certain point in your life, so you don't get distracted by things that don't help you reach your goals. You can learn to develop this level of focus from observing children at play. When a child is in the middle of a game and you call his name, he often doesn't hear you, because he is so deeply concentrating on the game.

What You Notice in the World Around You

We experience a whole world around us, but focus only on parts of it. There's a whole world around us that we sometimes don't even notice. Who knows what we are missing?

Try looking around you to see what you normally don't pay attention to, and notice if you see something that you didn't notice before. Since you will find many things that you now see when you really look, try seeing the good in others, if you haven't noticed it already. When your child or partner talks to you, look at his or her eyes and notice them, too. Since you now know that you are the one who interprets what you see, chose positive thoughts, so you will see what's positive in the world around you, which will make you feel happier, no matter what you do.

This experience of seeing and not seeing can affect your personal life and relationships. What you see can lead you to have certain experiences, while what you don't see can shape what you experience, too.

I had this experience in meeting my husband. The first time I met him was at a party in Tel-Aviv in January 1999. Later on, I found a picture from 1998 of me crossing Shenkin Street in Tel-Aviv, and the camera also caught his studio in that picture, before I even knew about his existence. In other words, he was in my life before I even knew or noticed.

Sometimes, I wonder how many times he had been near me before I finally noticed him at the party. Could it be that we had been at the beach at the same time when we were children without knowing? If we had noticed each other, maybe we might have met earlier. Or if I wasn't paying attention later on, maybe we would not have met at all. Have you ever wondered about things like this – about what you see or don't see and how it might shape your experience?

Another example of the way we see selectively is when you go someplace and see certain things but not others. Say you attend a seminar with 100 people, and after a month someone meets you and says that he saw you at the seminar, yet you never noticed him. Or vice versa, maybe you saw someone who didn't notice you.

The feelings you have about what you see, or the emotions triggered by that can shape your experiences and enable you to determine how you act or don't act. For example, one of my trainees said that the kitten saw the tiger because it wished to be brave like a tiger. Then, she shared that she was afraid of moving out of her comfort zone, indicating that she would like to be brave like the tiger. With her new self-awareness, it was now up to her to choose if she wanted to do something to get out of her comfort zone or not. Could she be brave and let go of her fear like the tiger as she wished, or would she hold on to her fear?

Should you be in a similar situation where you feel held back by your fear or other negative feelings that keep you from moving on, you need to work on letting go of your fear or getting rid of that negativity. One of the techniques I like to use to help my clients is Time Line Therapy® or TLT,® which is a great technique to let go of fear or any unwarranted negative emotion.

What about your own wants and feelings? Did what you write or see also reflect your inner wishes, desires, or even your fears? What can you do to move towards what you really desire and let go of any negative emotions in your life?

CHAPTER 3: USING PICTURES TO GAIN DEEPER INSIGHTS ABOUT YOURSELF

How Pictures Can Be a Source of Learning and Information

Pictures can be a valuable tool for learning about yourself and your goals, as well as gaining insights from and about others.

The notion that images can be a major source of insights and information dates back over 150 years. Sometimes the quote: "A picture is worth a thousand words" is traced back to Napoleon Bonaparte, who said "Un bon croquis vaut mieux qu'un long discours," which translates to "A good sketch is better than a long speech," a comment that politicians today are well aware of. While this comment by Napoleon is sometimes translated as "A picture is worth a thousand words," the phrase gained currency in the English language and particularly in the U.S. in the early 1900s, perhaps because of the spread of photography. For example, a 1911 newspaper article used the expression "Use a picture. It's worth a thousand words," and a 1913 newspaper ad announced: "One Look Is Worth a Thousand Words."

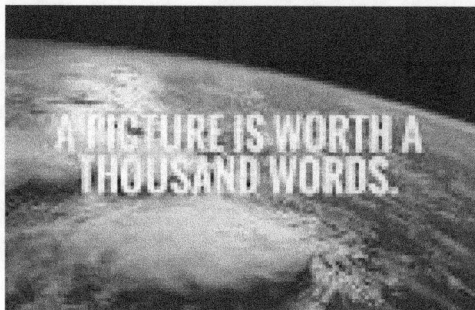

A PICTURE IS WORTH A THOUSAND WORDS.

Wherever the phrase originated, it is a very powerful tool for self-discovery and sharing ideas with others.

To illustrate, I have used the cat/tiger picture which has been very evocative for participants in my workshops, seminars, and lectures. You can use any picture that resonates with you to start an internal dialogue with yourself or with others.

What you see is a reflection of your state of mind, which includes your thoughts and feelings at the time, as well as any new insights you might have recently received or may need for your life now. You can use these images on your own to trigger associations and learn how these images can bring you insights and inspiration. Or you can gain additional information and wisdom by getting input from others, when they share how they interpret the picture they see.

Using This Image for Seeing Where You Are Now and in the Future

You can use images in multiple ways:
- You can look at them and see what first comes to mind, and then wait for subsequent thoughts to come, which are triggered by your previous thoughts.
- You can frame a question or series of questions in your mind as you approach each image. Ask the questions and then let the answers come to you in your thoughts or through visualizations.
- You can participate in a group experience where you jointly look at these images and see what comes to mind or bring a series of questions to the group. In asking these

questions, you can use your own list of written questions. Just ask them mentally or invite each person in the group to ask a question for everyone in the group to think about or visualize.

Your questions can include any time period from the past to the future. Some questions might be:

- What experiences does this image trigger from my past?
- What can I learn from this image about myself?
- What current situation does this image invite me to think about?
- What qualities do I see in the cat and tiger? Are these qualities I currently have or want for myself?
- What does this image tell me about what I would like to be or do in the future?
- What qualities of the cat and tiger would I like to develop in the future?

As you think about these issues or ask these questions, you might visualize yourself taking the necessary steps to achieve what you want.

Say you want to be a stronger, more confident, more powerful person, as reflected by the image of the tiger, and now you see yourself as the smaller, weaker cat lacking in power and confidence. Then, you can imagine projecting yourself from the cat into the tiger and visualize yourself having those qualities. You might feel the power flow through your veins; you might feel that added power and strength charging into you like electricity. Then, you might imagine what you would like to do when you have that additional power, such as building rapport with a boss who undervalues your abilities or getting more involved in community activities. The idea is to start with the image, use it to inform and inspire yourself, and then act on the positive ideas triggered by the image to create change and improvements in yourself.

When you participate in these activities on your own, you can write a record of your experiences and how you can put them into practice. Or if you are participating in these activities with another person or a group, you can set up a buddy system or group support network, where you share your experiences and encourage one another about what you can do.

CHAPTER 4: AN EXERCISE ON DISCOVERING WHO YOU WANT TO BE

Now that you better understand how to use the cat-tiger picture or other image that inspires you to learn more about yourself, you can ask yourself a series of questions to probe more deeply about who you are and what you want to be. Write down the answers as they come to you. Don't try to edit them or analyze whatever comes to you. Just let these insights guide your writing, because your first intuitive responses will be what come from your inner self or soul.

Is what I have seen in the picture a reflection of my life? How might it reflect where I am now?

_____

_____

_____

_____

_____

_____

Who is my true self? Who am I really?

_____

_____

_____

_____

_____

_____

_____

What are my fears? What holds me back? Ask yourself
four times: "Why is that a problem?" in order to get
down to the real problem.

_____

_____

_____

_____

_____

_____

_____

What am I curious about that will motivate me to overcome my fear? (Let's say you are afraid of flying, but are curious enough about touring Europe, then this will motivate you to overcome your fear.)

_____

_____

_____

_____

_____

_____

Now that you have made your list of things that you want to achieve, visualize, feel, and hear them, as if you have already obtained them. Imagine you are having that experience in the moment. The more you sense that this is real now, the more likely you are to achieve this goal and stay motivated. It is like a GPS. Once you put in the address, you are programed to get there.

Next, ask yourself more specifically about your goals for your work and personal life. Write down the first things that come to mind.

What do I want for my career? For my relationship? For my project? For my health and fitness? Family? Spirituality? Self-development? How much time do I spend on each daily? (Set some timelines for when you want to accomplish these different plans. Set a specific due date).

_____

_____

_____

_____

_____

_____

_____

Where am I now in my career, relationship, or project?

_____

_____

_____

_____

_____

_____

_____

Next to help motivate you to achieve your goal, ask yourself: "What will I gain when I have achieved something?" "How fantastic or proud will I feel?" List all the things that will make it worthwhile for you to overcome any fears and will motivate you enough to act. (For example, if you have stage fright, you might note that overcoming that fear will allow you to give lectures and people will pay for your expenses, enabling you to travel to new places.) Make what you want to do as compelling as possible to motivate you to achieve your desired goals.

_____

_____

_____

_____

_____

_____

How will I know when I have accomplished these goals, and what will I feel, see, or hear when I have done so? To answer these questions, close your eyes and imagine yourself in this future time when you have achieved these goals. Go ahead – feel it, see it, hear it now!!! Take about 3-5 minutes to fully experience this.

_____

_____

_____

_____

_____

_____

_____

What are the actual actions I am going to take in order to move from where I am now to where I want to be?

_____

_____

_____

_____

_____

_____

_____

At the end of this exercise, review your answers, and keep them with you to use as a daily reminder for the small steps you need to take every day to move towards achieving your goals.

CHAPTER 5: 35 INSIGHTS TO GUIDE YOUR PERSONAL DEVELOPMENT

Insights from the crowd can be very powerful, as individuals share what they have learned about themselves and others from viewing an image.

The following perspectives come from previous groups or individual clients I have trained using the cat/tiger picture. These learnings include insights about the self, others, and one's relationships with people.

Have Gratitude

As we imagined ourselves looking at the mirror like the cat does, I realized the importance of feeling gratitude for who we are or whatever we are experiencing. Therefore, I continually tell the attendees in my workshops, "When you look at yourself in the mirror, see the things that make you special. Be thankful for the qualities you have that make you YOU. See what is good about you and be grateful for what you have and for your ability to become even better." As Ben Zoma states in the Talmud, "Who is rich? The one who is happy with what he has."

Express Your Gratitude to Yourself and Others

When you feel thankful for something, it is important to recognize this feeling within yourself and share it with others, as well as not take anything for granted.

That's what I do. I want to be who I am, which for me includes strongly believing that G-d has made me who I am and continues to guide me. Since this belief has given me great joy and fulfillment, I share it with you, and I hope others will acknowledge the way G-d guides their own life.

One way I do this is by praising G-d in my own gratitude or when others share their success or gratitude with me. I do this to acknowledge the Creator's help in gaining the wisdom and success I or others have achieved.

As stated in the Bible in Deuteronomy:
> "You may say to yourself, 'My power and the strength of my hands have produced this wealth for me.' But remember the Lord your G-d, for it is He who gives you the ability to produce wealth, and so confirms His covenant, which He swore to your ancestors, as it is today." (Deuteronomy 8:17-18)

Remember How Unique You Are

There are all sorts of indicators that show how unique you are. At the airport they take your fingerprint to identify you, because nobody has the same fingerprint as you do. Some buildings now use eye recognition technology to enable people to open doors, because the pattern of colors and lines in our eyes is different for each person. The DNA of each person is unique, and no two people in the world are identical. Imagine how unique and special you are!

Be True to Yourself

Look at your eyes in the mirror, since the eyes are the window to your inner soul. No matter what the external factors, your eyes talk. So, looking at your eyes in the mirror is a good way to find the truth, when you ask questions about your best qualities and strengths or what you want to be, since your eyes will tell you the truth. Likewise, don't let others dissuade you from your truth once you know what it is. If your true self is that you love helping other people, ignore it when people try to put you down for doing what you want to do, such as spending time doing volunteer work for poor people, rather than going to big social events you find dull. Don't become who others want you to be. Stay loyal to your own inner self.

Recognize Your Wishes

In being true to yourself, recognize what you really want and be guided by those things, when you set your goals and take action based on your goals. When I listened to clients lamenting about their overwhelming schedules, I realized that while you should respect the wishes and demands of others, you should also honor your own wishes. Sometimes we are pulled by so many distractions from our work and by the demands and needs of others, that we forget to pay enough attention to what we want and who we want to become. It is perfectly legitimate to fulfill your own needs, too, since fulfilling your own needs will give you more strength and power, which will help you in helping others.

The image of the tiger teaches you to give time to yourself to grow and become the tiger or lion you want to be. You want to care about others, and you have a responsibility to take care of yourself, too.

In fulfilling this responsibility to take care of yourself, you shouldn't let any person tell you who you are, just as you shouldn't tell others who they are and how they should be. Rather, decide who you are for yourself, and use the mirror to help you do this as you look at your image. You need to be yourself for your ultimate happiness.

Taking Feedback

Learn from feedback to improve yourself. By doing so, you are not changing your true self or undermining your purpose. Rather, this feedback is helping you be better at who you are and can help you overcome bad habits. You are here for a greater purpose, and you must recognize that you are here to give value to others, too, so you can't do things that intentionally hurt anyone else.

Sometimes you need to overcome bad habits or unconscious impulses; then you need to find the good attributes within yourself, so you can choose to be those instead. Overcoming bad habits and impulses can take time. But if you believe that you can overcome and do everything in your power to get rid of these negative qualities in yourself, then YES, YOU CAN!!!

Exercise Your Free Choice

A number of the trainees who looked at the cat-tiger image said they learned from the picture that you can choose how to look at yourself. That's because the cat isn't limited to seeing the image of a cat in the mirror; it can choose to see what it wants, which is the powerful tiger with the various qualities different people attribute to him. Likewise, you can choose how to look at life in general and how to respond to circumstances or situations.

My mother-in-law tells me that her mom used to tell her that she would never get married because of a scar she got near her eyes. She chose to ignore her mom's remark, called her scar a "dimple" and considered it something nice. It's a good thing that she chose to look at herself with this very positive approach, because she later got married to a man who considered her beautiful, too, just as she saw herself.

Seeing What You Need to Learn at the Time

After noticing that everyone perceived the images and what they learned about themselves differently, I learned that everyone responded to their specific reality -- the particular image in front of them -- by seeing what they needed to learn at that moment. This realization was reflected in the "aha" moments which many people had, as they noticed what the image triggered in themselves. They recognized the image was telling them truths about their mind set and what they needed to know to help them improve their day to day lives.

Discovering What Holds You Back and Letting Go

As people shared their experiences with the tiger image and how they met resistance in expanding themselves and achieving their bigger goals, I explained why things may hold us back from becoming who we want to be. For example, some people may think a scar makes them unlovable, so that belief holds them back from meeting a spouse, in contrast to my mother-in-law who chose to see the scar as an attractive dimple.

When we hold ourselves back because of fear, we might be sorry later, as I learned when I asked older people what they regret in life. Many were sorry about what they didn't do or accomplish rather than what they did. However, there is no point in regretting the past; it is better to learn from it, let go of it, and look ahead to what one can do next. At the same time, we can use the knowledge of others' regrets to propel ourselves forward.

Sometimes our past experiences that we allow to limit us in the present or future keep us from being the best we can be. These experiences might be attached to negative emotions we felt or to something we interpreted incorrectly. As an example, maybe we were singing when our parents wanted to focus on something else and therefore told us to "hush up." But instead of recognizing our parents had other concerns at the time, we concluded that we sang terribly, did something stupid or weren't important to them. Then we carry this misconception or limiting belief about our abilities and don't dare to sing in front of people again.

It is therefore vital that you let go of any negative feelings associated with what occurred in the past. Instead, focus on learning about who and what you are now and what you hope to be in the future. By letting go of these negative emotions from your past, you open yourself up to learning from them instead.

Letting go is vital, because your subconscious (or unconscious) mind and nervous system runs automatically, just as your respiration is involuntary. When you don't let go, these negative feelings remain in your subconscious mind, and since more than 90% of the time you operate from your subconscious mind, you don't want any negative emotions there, influencing the way you feel and act.

Thus, get rid of any traumas, limiting beliefs, or bad decisions that you made in the past. You are often not conscious of them, because they are stored in your subconscious mind and you can't recall them consciously. They could come from way back in your past, say from the time you were three years old and even much earlier. You consciously "forgot" about these bad experiences, but unconsciously they are limiting you as you go forward.

Luckily, you can retrieve these repressed negative experiences, let go of them, and get new learning by using various powerful techniques, such as taught in NLP and Time Line Therapy®

To illustrate how deeply something that you carry from your past can affect your life today, I will share a story of how I helped one of my clients. The client expressed a frustration about her life. She complained that no matter how hard she worked and how talented she was, she never made money or had enough money.

When we did the TLT® process on her, she recalled an incident when she was a little girl and her parents had a huge fight about what to do with the money they had made. That fight was traumatic for her, so as a child, she decided that money was rotten because it created fights. No wonder she couldn't make money because she had such a limiting belief in her unconscious mind. Only when she got a different interpretation of what had happened and a new learning about how she wrongly generalized that all money is associated with fights could she let go. For now, she could see the positive qualities of money, and as a result, she could finally have a good relationship with it. After this process, she met an investor, and for the first time she didn't scare him away. He invested in her start-up company.

Forgive Others

As part of letting go, learn to forgive others. The importance of doing so is illustrated in this story from the Jewish sages. After two men argued about something, one slapped the other. The other man wrote on the sand, "My friend slapped me." Soon after that, the man who was slapped almost drowned in the water, and the friend who slapped him saved him. This time the man who was slapped wrote what his friend did on a stone: "My friend saved me."

The friend then asked the man he slapped and then saved, why his friend had written about what happened on the sand and the second time on the stone.

62

The man then answered him: "I wrote on the sand to forget something bad and to forgive. I wrote on the stone to remember something good."

Let the negative emotions of the bad things that you experience from others fly away like sand in the wind by forgiving. At the same time, embrace the good emotions and preserve them when something good happens. Engrave them in the hard stone of your memory in order to remember these good experiences in the future.

Bring Up Positive Memories

Bring positive memories and pictures from your past into the present to uplift your spirits, have good feelings about yourself, or remember the things you love to do.

Accessing these positive memories is also a powerful motivational tool. In NLP, we often use anchoring, a technique to recall a good time from the past when we felt really good and inspired. For now, recall a time when you felt totally motivated, loved, or powerful, or a combination of these feelings.

You can use the list below to trigger your memories of a happy time from the past. Keep it handy, such as in your wallet or bag, so you can take it out whenever you need an injection of motivation. Then, just remember whatever comes to you and feel good.

List those times when you were totally happy. What did you see, feel, hear?
List those times when you were totally confident/inspired/ loved/motivated. What did you see, feel, hear?

_____

_____

_____

_____

_____

_____

_____

Have Courage to Overcome Unwarranted Fears

When one woman viewed the cat-tiger image, she mentioned that she sometimes felt scared and would like to be brave like the tiger in the picture. Sometimes the best way to be courageous and cope with your fear is to do what you are afraid of doing, and you might find out that it is not as scary as you thought.

For example, people who feared flights or speaking in front of people found that by forcing themselves to do what they feared, they were no longer afraid of doing those things anymore. That's because once you choose to confront your fear, you become bigger, stronger, and more powerful, as your fear shrinks in size. So be courageous if you fear something. As you look at the mirror and see the tiger or lion you wish to be, say to yourself: "I can do it!" Repeat the words like an affirmation, and these words will empower you and help you to be brave. You will feel your own courage increase as you say the words.

What if you are afraid to aspire to something bigger out of fear of failure or disappointment? Sometimes we are afraid we might fail, so we don't try something new or different. Sometimes life forces us to confront these fears. Can you imagine not going to school out of fear of failing tests? Normally, you still have to go despite your fear. And you want to overcome that fear, because it will hold you back from advancing in life and fulfilling your dreams.

A good practice to overcome this fear is to visualize, hear, and feel the future you as the successful person you will become, and focus on that instead of your fear. People learn from their failures. Think of how many times Thomas Edison failed at creating the lightbulb before he finally succeeded.

Another common fear to overcome is the fear of what other people think of you. Rather than worry about what others may think about who you are or have been, concentrate on what you now want to become. Once you develop this vision who you will become and act to change yourself to fulfill that vision, people will come to have a new image of you, based on your future image of yourself. Some of the most successful people have gained their success by creating this future vision of themselves having achieved their dream.

Mirror Others to Identify and Overcome Your Fears

This technique involves selecting others to be models for your behavior and mirroring or acting like they might in a particular situation. As an example of how it works, someone looks in the mirror, while he thinks that he wants to be brave or inspiring like someone else. Or he seeks to possess any other characteristics that he feels he is lacking and someone else has. These characteristics may be very different, even opposite the qualities he has now, which is why we often say that opposites attract. We are drawn to people with qualities we don't have, or we can develop those qualities for ourselves.

For example, when you are afraid, it is reassuring to know that you have someone near you who is brave enough to protect you, though you may want to develop that bravery and ability to protect yourself. While you can actually look in a mirror and visualize the person with the qualities you want to develop, you can do this mentally, because with your mirror neurons you can identify with something you wish to have but are afraid to act to obtain it. Then, you can mentally mirror the behavior of the other person with the desired qualities, as though you are acting that way yourself. In this way, you can identify with other people to understand their actions, and can learn the skills they have by watching and modeling them until these new abilities become part of you.

When you admire someone, ask yourself, "What is it that I admire so much about someone else?" or "Why do I feel so good when I'm watching him?" This way, you will become more self-aware of your desires and what you want to improve. If you are afraid and keep watching someone who is bravely doing what you want to do, you can "borrow" the courage to do it, too.

This ability to overcome fear by watching others is something you can often see in the way children behave. Fearful children see other kids easily jump into the swimming pool. When they see that these other children are safe, they are likely to overcome their fear and jump in, too.

Thus, one way to get over your fears is using someone you appreciate who has overcome a similar adversity as a model. Let's say you admire a big motivational speaker, this might indicate that you would like to become more inspiring yourself. Howard Stern, on the popular TV show, *America's Got Talent*, says that he most admires what he fears the most. He confesses that he is the most fearful person and therefore admires others who are not afraid. Thus, as he explains, when he sees people do scary things for a minute or two, such as jump high in the air over a flaming pit, he can feel brave for that time, as if he has done those things himself. By modeling you will eventually become braver yourself.

Have Curiosity to Overcome Fear

Another way to get over your fear is to replace it with curiosity, just as children do. Their curiosity is commonly stronger than their fear. They tend to ignore or overcome the fear and continue doing something, which generally helps them learn new things and makes them stronger. This is how they acquire a new skill or gain the independence to do something on their own. Certainly, they need to exercise common sense, and being cautious will protect them in the case of true danger, such as pulling away from the heat on a stove to avoid getting burned. Sometimes moving out from your comfort zone, such as moving to a new place, might seem scary, but if you are curious enough to try something new and exciting, you will overcome your fear.

Use an Affirmation to Overcome Fear

Affirming that you can do something is a good way to overcome fear. Just tell yourself over and over that you can do something, and you will find that you can.

The affirmation, "We are all the same or equal," is a good exercise to practice if you fear being with others in different settings, such as if you fear meeting people in a new crowd or networking at business events. Or suppose you worry what people will say about you or are afraid to speak in front of a crowd. When you remind yourself that we are all human beings, we all want to be loved, and you are as good as and equal to others, this self-talk will help you overcome your fear of being judged. Also, remember that when you speak in front of a crowd, it's not just about you but about your helping others with your message.

Recognize that G-d Is Behind You

Another insight from this picture is that G-d is there to help and support us, as expressed in the Bible saying that "G-d is our Shepherd" (Psalms 23). This insight of G-d's support is reflected in the cat seeing the much larger tiger in the mirror, because sometimes when you look in the mirror, you can see and know that someone much bigger than you, is behind you, much like the cat seeing the much bigger tiger. Recognize that our Father, the Creator, is watching you, so don't be afraid. He is there to help you. Trust G-d because G-d is behind you!!!

What You See Becomes Your Reality

"What you see or imagine becomes your reality" is another truth which is reflected in the cat-tiger image, because if you see yourself as bigger and stronger, you will most likely make that your reality. Here is a fun exercise that will show you how what you think creates your reality.

Hold your arms straight in front of you parallel to each other. Now imagine you are holding something really heavy in your right hand, and your left hand is pulled up by a kite. Next, close your eyes and feel the weight in your right hand. When you open your eyes, look at your arms and see what happened. If you truly imagined holding the weight, even for a few seconds, when you opened your eyes, your hands weren't parallel to each other anymore. Instead, your right hand was lower than the left hand because it feels heavier due to the weight. That's because your imagination affected your physiology and behavior.

69

This exercise illustrates that you will become what you imagine, because the mind can turn what you imagine into your reality. That is why we start to itch when someone talks to us about lice or our mouth waters when someone talks about a food we like. Many trainers say, "The mind doesn't differentiate between reality and imagination," which is their way of saying that what you imagine can be so "real" that it physically affects you and your behavior.

Likewise, it is good to imagine and visualize the positive way in which you want to grow and develop to become what you want to be a year or two from now. When you do this, your mind reads what you visualize as reality, just as you might experience a reality in the movies, leading you to act to make what you imagined a current reality or change what you viewed into a different reality.

As an example, a middle-aged woman client called me after she watched a movie in which an old man only dated young women. As she watched, she believed for a moment that this might be her reality – that she was no longer attractive to males, because they all preferred younger women, so she would never find a man to marry her. But I led her to change her interpretation, on the basis that the movie was only about one older man, and she could remove this belief that she wouldn't find a man. She just needed to use an exercise in which she would replace her negative belief with a positive one that she would appeal to a man.

In short, if you believe you can have it, you can; if you don't believe you can, you won't. So, try it. Think about what you want in your own life; believe you can have it; take the action steps to actualize it; and you will eventually make what you believe real. As the American sociologist, William Isaac Thomas (1863-1947) has stated, "If men define situations as real, they are real in their consequences."

Recognizing the Two Sides of Yourself

Many mirrors have two sides – one where you see yourself as you are, the other which magnifies your reflection – commonly at a 3:1 or 5:1 ratio. The lesson from recognizing the mirror's two sides is to learn to use the relevant side for your best growth at this moment. The usual mirror shows you as you are now. The magnifying mirror shows a much larger vision of yourself, which might be how you want to be as you grow and expand your presence to others.

Remember to always look at the relevant side of the mirror that serves you for your best growth at the time. Where you are now is the regular side, and where you want to be as you grow and improve yourself is the magnifying side. By knowing this gap between your present and future self, you can decide what steps to take to get where you want to go.

Don't Magnify Your Faults, Only Your Strengths

Looking at the magnifier mirror also reminds you to not magnify your faults. Sometimes when we look at ourselves to see how we are doing, we criticize ourselves because we exaggerate our faults. In doing so, we are using the magnifier mirror to look for our faults, so we magnify them.

For example, a woman might say: "Oh, no. My face looks so tired and wrinkled," leading her to cut back on her many activities. If she concentrated instead on seeing herself effectively perform various activities from working at a computer to hiking with friends, she would remind herself of the person she can be. She would focus on her abilities and strengths, and then she would naturally express them in the real world, thereby turning her vision into reality. Therefore, when you look in the mirror focus on the best parts of yourself – your strengths, your beauty, your abilities – so you can change your own reality into a better positive one.

Don't Be Egotistical or Judgmental

A few of the viewers thought that the kitten had too large of an ego in seeing itself as a much larger tiger. I find that this feedback is a reminder that you shouldn't be egotistical, since that keeps you away from your success and learning. This barrier to success and learning occurs when you think you know it all. Also, ego may lead you to think you don't owe anybody anything, so that unless you get something in return, you won't share and refer your clients to others who might help them with something which you don't do. Or ego may lead you to feel vengeful, if you feel someone hasn't given you what you deem is the appropriate respect. The problem with being egotistical is that egotists don't want others to succeed, because they think that others' success would detract from their own. They tend to find or magnify faults in others, wrongly believing that putting down others will make them look better.

Such negative thoughts and actions commonly backfire, because, as the popular saying goes, "What goes around comes around." Accordingly, when these negative attitudes occur, that can ruin any relationship and hurt growth.

You can see many examples of the problems many people experience when they are too egotistical or judgmental. On reality TV shows like "Survivor," when someone has a big ego, they are often unlikeable and are voted off first. So, don't be egotistical. Be more acceptable instead. Treat people favorably and fairly, and others will generally treat you favorably and fairly in return.

Staying Humble

As much as you want to believe in yourself, it is also important to stay humble. This is another bit of wisdom I have learned from the cat-tiger picture. Looking through the mirror, you may see yourself as a tiger; but don't forget to stay as humble as the cat.

It is very easy to fall into the trap of ego and be overly proud of yourself. It is important, of course, to acknowledge what you have done and celebrate your victories, such as by rewarding yourself, and remind yourself that you earned this acknowledgment.

Yet, while patting yourself on the back and rewarding yourself, remember to stay humble, too, because there is only one G-d. Unfortunately, when people idolize themselves, they might hurt others, look down at people, or become possessive, which will generally lead to repercussions in the future. In other words, do work on improving yourself and branding the "you" who you are now and are becoming, so you allow people to see in you what you see in yourself. At the same time, stay humble, so you become kinder and see the light in others. This compassion for others should become a part of your self-identity and branding, too.

Avoid Confrontations

Sometimes you may find that people make you angry, because they have done something you feel is wrong, hurtful, or inappropriate to you or someone you care about. You may feel you want to strike back at them in return like a tiger. It is better that you don't retaliate. You might escalate the situation and make it worse. If you respond when you are upset, you might say or do things that you will later regret. It is better to wait for things to calm down, if you want to speak with them to try to resolve the issue.

You don't want to create enemies. In fact, it is generally better to avoid a confrontation, much like someone in a road rage situation is best advised to walk away rather than engage with someone who is already angry and could strike back in dangerous and unpredictable ways.

Let Others Be Who They Are

Everyone sees different things in the mirror. You should recognize the uniqueness in others, just as you want others to recognize the uniqueness in you. It is important to let other people be who they are. That means family members, too.

Let your kids be who they are rather than expecting them to conform to your expectations of what you want them to be.

Be Honest With Yourself About What You Have to Do to Make Changes

When you look at yourself in the mirror, only you know who you are. So be honest with yourself. If you know that you need help and support, and that you need to make a positive change in your life, then take the help you need and JUST DO IT.

Be Kind and Patient with Yourself and Others

Any kind of change takes time, so be kind and patient. Recognize that you may make mistakes and stumble from time to time along the way, so don't be judgmental and accept that it is part of your learning and growth. Not making mistakes means not doing anything, which is a poor choice. The only way to progress is by learning from your mistakes. Then, move on and be ready to take on the next challenge. For support in remaining kind and patient, pray to G-d to guide and help you stay kind, give to others, be compassionate, and be concerned about others.

Seeing Yourself the Way You Want to Be Seen

The mirror image also teaches us to see ourselves as we want to be seen, just as the cat wants to be seen as a powerful tiger. The mirror functions this way, because what you see in yourself, other people will see in you, too.

Therefore, be conscious about how you look at yourself. Even if you have to pretend for a while in order to feel confident, act as if you already have that confidence, and eventually, you will feel that way.

Athletes use this "see yourself as you want to be seen" approach in their training. In addition to practicing physically, they are likely to practice a skill in their imagination. Researchers have found that imagined practice does improve their performance. For instance, a golfer may practice a swing on the green and later repeat that same skill mentally. As long as the stroke in the imagined practice is correct, that pre-visualization will help him later when he goes out on the course. Likewise, actors may practice their lines mentally as well as on stage, resulting in a better performance when it is time to actually perform before an audience.

Visualize Your Wishes

Since reality mirrors what goes on in your mind, whenever you wish for something, visualize yourself having it, just like the Wright brothers wanted to fly and they did. As a result, if you visualize your wishes about what you want to become, even though these wishes do not reflect who you are yet, you will become what you wish. Visualize big and you will more likely become that. You can also better achieve the goal you visualize by looking for the support of G-d and feeling you have G-d's blessing for what you are doing.

Sharing Your Learnings from the Picture with Others

Besides learning about yourself from the cat-tiger picture – or any other picture that resonates with you, you can share any wisdom you have learned with others. I have shared my own insights and the insights of others who have viewed this picture. Through sharing, you can learn much more as you look at yourself and your relationship with others in your personal life, at work, and in the community. So, share your wisdom, learnings and experiences with others as well as using this wisdom and what you learn and experience for your own personal growth.

How to Find Out Who You Are

When you learn about yourself through a picture, you get all kinds of hints and clues that can help you find your inner light, purpose, and other things about yourself. To learn these answers, as you look in the mirror, ask yourself: "Who am I?" "What are my strengths?" and "What excites me so much that adrenaline rushes keep me from sleeping?" You may find there are a number of things that excite you. For instance, at the core of your love of adventure, travel, and exploration is a desire to discover and experience new things. Once you know what you like, you will enjoy life more and radiate that enjoyment to others.

You may also learn that different things excite you at different times. These are all hints about your true purpose. Take these hints and change your thoughts about your purpose in a way that you feel excited about what you want to do or create. Then, take this inspiration to the world in the form of a product, service, or activity which you want to create.

That's what happened to me, since the catalyst for this book was my excitement after I gave a presentation to entrepreneurial women and inspired them to get the best out of their uniqueness and passions. When I came home, I couldn't fall asleep because I was so happy. I had felt great joy because I found my own true purpose in sharing my insights with these women. It feels so good to be true to yourself and do what you love the most. Then, it is easy to do whatever you are doing on an even bigger scale, which for me involves sharing my messages with larger and larger groups of people around the world.

Finding Your Inner Spark

Another insight from this picture is that as the cat sees her inner tiger, the tiger is like our inner spark, which is something we all want to find. This inner spark might be lit by many things that excite us, much like a match might light a candle wick, which lights up the whole room. One way to light this spark is by being a good influence on others.

Tell and remind yourself of the actions that help to light your inner spark as you look in the mirror. These are the things that make you happy and joyous, and consequently you spread those feelings to the world around you.

Finding Your Inner Light and Fulfilling Your Purpose

To help you stay loyal to your inner self, remind yourself who you are and how precious you are, as you look at yourself in the mirror or when you talk to yourself. This reminder is also a key to finding your true purpose which is linked to your inner self, which is derived from your creation by G-d. In turn, this linkage has been reflected in recent scientific research, in which researchers found that the patterns appearing within a certain segment of each person's DNA corresponded to the Hebrew word for G-d in the Bible (http://dailycurrant.com/2013/02/01/message-god-hidden- dna-sequence)

This latest finding of seeing the imprint of G-d's name in our DNA helps to demonstrate that you are not alone, since you have G-d within you. These findings also are a reminder and motivation to discover your inner light to fulfill your purpose. They have certainly helped me reaffirm my purpose in helping others discover these truths, since I figure that if G-d has imprinted His name in my DNA, He probably has high expectations for me. So, I should do my best to make Him proud in his kingdom.

In other words, the very DNA which has made you who you are shows that you are created by G-d and in His image. Therefore, to fulfill your destiny, seek your inner light to fulfill your purpose and share what you are here to do with the whole world. Then, by having high expectations for yourself and fulfilling your purpose, you not only feel great joy for what you have achieved, but you also make G-d proud of His creation -- YOU.

Enjoying Life More When You Find Your Purpose

Once you find your true purpose so that you do work that you are deeply passionate about, you will no longer experience what you are doing as work. That's because you are having fun, doing what you want and ought to do. You gain great joy, when you think about how many people you have helped by sharing your unique passion, wisdom, and expertise with the world. Besides enjoying life more, you will continually create a better world for yourself and those around you, which will bring you even more enjoyment.

So, ask yourself the following questions to find this purpose and experience more joy in your life: "What do you like to do the most?" "What makes you feel fulfilled and happy?"

_____

_____

_____

_____

_____

_____

_____

Sharing Your True Purpose with Others

Once you find out your true purpose, share it with others. You can do it in various ways. One way is to do it more personally on a face-to-face basis. An alternative is to go to your computer and write down the wisdom you have gained and share it with the world, such as in a book, in lectures, on blogs, in the social media, in one-on-one communications, or in the therapy you provide to people who need your help.

***

Now that you have deeper insights, you can go back to some of the questions you've worked on in previous chapters and see if you want to modify, make changes, or add anything. Make sure that you cover the following:

- What do you want to achieve in each aspect of your life? Be specific and state your answer positively; also write down due dates to accomplish each goal

- Where are you currently (in all aspects of life – in work, your personal life, and in finding balance between the two?

- Check that your goal is achievable, that you gave yourself enough time to achieve it, and that what you want to do doesn't hurt anyone. If you find any problems with achieving your goal, go back and find another goal or goals to work on.

- What actions or steps you are going to take in order to achieve you goal?

- Know how it feels when you have accomplished your goal. Imagine it as if you have already achieved it a few minutes after the due date for this accomplishment.

CHAPTER 6: TAKING RESPONSIBILTY FOR YOURSELF

One of the keys to your success is taking responsibility for yourself and not blaming others for your setbacks or failures. You are looking at yourself in the mirror.

Don't Blame Others for Things You Do

If there are things you don't like about yourself or you experience some setbacks or failures along the way to achieving your goals, don't blame others for what you don't like about yourself or as an excuse for your failures. You need to be in charge and take the responsibility for making the changes and the improvements needed in your life, because responsibility lies in taking control of your own life.

Take Responsibility

When you take responsibility, you acknowledge your own role in contributing to any mistake or failure, and you also realize you can change or grow from what occurred. When you are responsible, you are in charge – so you can shape what happens next. That's why there is no thing such as failure when you take the long view, instead of focusing on whatever has gone wrong in the here and now. Rather, see any failure, mistake, or setback as another source of feedback for learning, mending, and getting better.

We all make mistakes and we have to be aware of them, so we can correct and do better next time. We can ask for forgiveness if these mistakes affected others, too. Then, having accepted responsibility from these mistakes and learning from them, we can move on.

How Blaming Others Can Limit You

When you blame others, you limit yourself, because you are telling yourself that someone else needs to fix your life. You might wait forever for someone to do this. Often people blame their unfortunate past for their current situation. They blame their past for what they lack in the present and use their bad experience as a reason for not succeeding now or in the future. By looking back to the past for excuses, they don't let themselves move forward with their dreams. They avoid creating a new life for themselves. One reason for this is that they still believe what they were told in their past, such as being told negative things about themselves that undermine their confidence and ability to succeed. For instance, they might come to believe they can't do anything on their own or are losers, because of statements they have heard from their parents, teachers, family members, and peers.

To illustrate, a client of mine felt miserable and blamed her husband for her stagnation in life. Rather than taking charge and progressing in her life, she found someone else to blame (her husband) and used him as a reason for why she couldn't find fulfillment. This is a good example of how blaming others can limit you. The client also blamed her husband for not appreciating her. As a result, she was in a conflict over whether she should stay with him or divorce him.

After she went through the process of seeing the cat/tiger image and asking questions to go deeper into herself, she came to realize there was no conflict or problem with her husband. Rather, she realized that her higher intention was self-fulfillment, and the problem was within herself. She couldn't access this truth about herself before. It was only after the session where she accessed and communicated with her unconscious mind that she realized that her lack of self-appreciation was what was really frustrating and upsetting her. She didn't appreciate herself, because she wasn't seeking the self-fulfillment, she wanted through exercising her skills.

She had come in crying, and she left smiling, because now she knew and trusted herself to go after the self-fulfillment, she really wanted by using her skills. As a result, she stopped blaming her husband for her unhappiness, realizing that it wasn't his fault that she wasn't taking care of herself. She stopped criticizing him, and instead she took the next steps to make herself happier by engaging in the activities she wanted to pursue to fulfill her newfound purpose. Once she got back in charge of her life and took the responsibility for her self-fulfillment, she projected appreciation, so not only did she experience acceptance and appreciation from her peers, but she felt appreciated by her husband, as well.

Use Your Self-Understanding to Get Out of an Unsupportive Environment

A big benefit of understanding yourself, recognizing who you are, and realizing your true worth is that you can get out of abusive or destructive relationships, whether in your personal life or at work. As I have found in talking to clients, when they gain confidence and recall their worth, abilities, and capabilities, they have the strength to get out of very destructive relationships.

They are able to walk away from relationships with abusers. If you encounter abusers in your own life, you will find that abusers are generally projecting their own flaws and failings onto you. A person may say you are jealous, and you know you are not. But they are jealous of you, so they say this false statement about you. In response, you might feel a desire to show them up for lying about you due to their jealousy, because they wish they had or could do something which you have or can do. Rather than getting sucked into playing their game, gracefully stay away from or leave such relationships.

Make Careful Decisions

When you hope to leave an unsupportive environment, make any decision and act in a careful and responsible way. For instance, if you don't like your boss or work and decide that you want to leave your job, consider different scenarios, so you can make a wise decision about what to do. Further consider how you will earn an income until you find another job. Maybe it is better to find another job before you leave.

When you make a decision like quitting a job that could have serious consequences, have an alternative plan, so you don't hurt yourself, your children, or others depending on you.

Think About How to Improve the Situation

Sometimes an unsupportive environment may be that way, because people treat you the way you treat yourself or allow them to treat you. As a result, you are contributing to the difficult situation by your own lack of ability to take charge of what is happening and shaping the situation.

When you look at the current situation, rather than walking away from it, first think about how to improve it. Is there any change of attitude that you can make that will cause others to be kinder to you or otherwise treat you better?

In confronting any difficult situation and deciding what to do, try to look at the picture in an objective way. One way to do this is to put yourself in the place of the person who bothers you to see his or her point of view. Let's say the boss keeps screaming at you and you feel cowed by his actions and resentful and angry, so you feel like quitting on the spot. Instead, if you pretend to be the boss yourself, you might discover the pressure that the boss has from the CEO, or you might notice that the employees don't collaborate, or they come to work only to get their paycheck at the end of the month, rather than being motivated to do their job well. You might also feel the stress that the boss goes through. Then, as a result of looking at the workplace from the boss's viewpoint, you may feel motivated to help improve the situation. As a result, the next day you come to work full of energy to get things done at a faster pace, or you may think of some time-saving procedures to help the employees work together more effectively. In turn, the boss will truly appreciate you, when he sees your extra effort, and now he praises you, rather than screaming at you. You may even get a promotion for doing such a good job.

Phrase Your Statements about Yourself in Positive Terms

Treat yourself like you expect others to treat you and speak to you. When you talk about your qualities or what you can do or have achieved, use positive phrasing. Rather than talk about what you don't do anymore, talk about what you will do from now on.

Also avoid disparaging phrases like "I'm so stupid" or defensive negating statements like "I'm not stupid," because your mind "hears" first the word "stupid" and only then it can negate it. It is better to talk in positive terms about the qualities you want to develop, such as saying: "I'm becoming more aware and perceptive," "I know more now about what to do," or "I'm getting smarter every day."

Talk about what you do see or understand. Use positive statements as much as possible.

Remind Yourself that You Love and Appreciate Yourself

Whatever you say can shape what you think and see, so use positive affirmations to feel more positive about yourself and whatever is happening in your life. When I gave birth, I used the affirmation "I love myself. I'm capable of giving birth. I will be a good loving mother." These thoughts helped me get through the fear and the challenge of a new experience.

Use positive statements to remind yourself that you love and appreciate YOU. Saying the words will help you think and feel them, and this will help to empower you whenever you face a challenging situation.

The Importance of Understanding Your Clients and Customers

When you understand your clients and customers, you are better able to recognize what they need and fulfill them. This means looking at the world from their point of view. Many people don't do this, so they have less success. Even people who are in the business of giving service to clients, like realtors, don't always understand the people they are dealing with, so they lose sales.
They try to sell their clients on something they think would be good for the client, rather than something the client wants. If they instead would go into their client's world and look at things from their client's perspective, they will have happier clients and sell more houses.

As part of developing this understanding, it is important to build rapport. A good way to do this is to mirror and match your client, so the client feels that he is watching himself in the mirror. If the client speaks slowly, be respectful and speak slowly, too.
This will help the client feel more comfortable with you, since people tend to like people who are similar to

themselves. Building rapport creates this feeling of mutual liking. You are in tune with the client, with the result that the client feels you are considerate and caring. You have made the effort to develop this bond

I had a student realtor who took my NLP for Business class. He told me that he always stayed calm and self-controlled and never got into the clients' moods, even when his clients were excited. After taking the class, he reported that he started to be excited with his clients and that increased his sales dramatically.

CHAPTER 7: TRAINING OTHERS

Once you have peered deep within, have examined who you really are, and what you need to do for your success, consider how to share your ideas with others and teach what you have learned. The following insights will provide you with guidelines to build courage to take action like the cat which turns into tiger.

Don't Wait to Be Perfect

No one can be completely perfect, so don't wait to be perfect. You gain progress and become better and better as you swim in the water. Seeking perfection will only delay your progress. You will find that people who wait to look perfect or speak perfectly don't progress enough, because they keep waiting for an unrealizable goal of being perfect. As a result, they are frozen in time, and this concern with being perfect leads to procrastination. The person thinks: "I will do it when I'm perfect." Meanwhile, others are progressing, and the person can lose the opportunities that come up, due to thinking "I can't do it. I'm not perfect enough yet." Rather than waiting until you are perfect, concentrate on giving value to others.

Seek to Train Others

Once you know where you are going, what you want to teach, and acquire the mandatory requirements or certifications, this is an ideal time to teach and train others. When I completed my training in NLP and acquired the certifications of practitioner, master, and trainer, I was encouraged to train and certify others. By training, you provide others with information to help them, and you get the best training for yourself at the same time. That's because you have to learn what you are doing even better than if you are only teaching yourself. You are working to pass this information on to others, and you want your students to master the material. So, you become even more skilled at whatever you are sharing with others. Plus, you are always learning from the students and their experiences and improving yourself every time. You become an expert as you practice more and teach more.

Some people will never do things before they think they are perfect, so they resist starting to speak, lecture, conduct workshops, present webinars, and train others for that reason. Just like delaying doing other things, your efforts to teach and train others won't happen, if you wait to become perfect. People who won't take the first step to share what they learn commonly give all kinds of excuses. They are usually resisting due to fear that they don't know enough. However, you never know enough; there is always more to learn. So, share what you know so far. Get started and you will learn much more yourself.

When you teach others, they become able to teach others, too. It's the same thing that happens when you teach your children; they later teach their children, and when you teach them well, this contributes to creating a better world. You and the children you teach are creating this better world for the future generations. As the Talmud says: "When you teach your son, you teach your son's son."

Encourage Yourself to Do More

If you start fearing that you are not ready to coach others, become a speaker, or run a seminar, then talk to and encourage yourself. Engaging in positive self-talk, along with finding a mentor and consulting with others, are especially good practices when you are a beginning coach or trainer of anything. Being in a supportive environment, such as joining a mastermind group, can help, too. Even being a beginner can be a big plus, because you are likely to be motivated to do even more for your prospective students, such as spending more time with them for a reduced price or giving them a complementary mentoring to show that you know what you are doing.

It can help you become a better teacher or coach when you have become very successful in your field, if you always act towards your prospective students kindly and humbly, as if you are a beginner. Then, too, it helps to give them more than they expect, as expressed in the common expression: "Promise more and give even more." Successful salespeople do this all the time, and the result is a very satisfied customer, because they have received more benefits than they thought they would get.

CHAPTER 8: USING PICTURES WITH A GROUP

Styles of Training, Coaching, Teaching, and Speaking

Once you start training others, consider the different styles of training you might use. In this book I covered using images in the training. I have found, and I'm sure you are convinced by now, that using pictures is a captivating approach, because you talk to each person in his or her language as pictures are universal and at the same time very personal. You get to reach each individual's heart, and each individual gains his own learning and perceptions from the picture. In this way, using images helps to create an intimate bond between the teacher and learner, which helps to reinforce whatever you are teaching.

As it says in the Bible:
"Train up a child in the way he should go: and when he is old, he will not depart from it."
(Proverbs 22:6).

Thus, you want to talk to your audience in a way that you can reach each person, based on that person's way of relating to what you teach.

Using pictures is an ideal way to do this, since the image lasts longer in your prospect's mind than a series of words. It is more dramatic and compelling, and therefore more memorable. A good example is using the periodic table to learn the elements in chemistry, since this table illustrates vividly the different elements, rather than a student seeing them listed in a long paragraph. Likewise, if your math or economics teacher used diagram to show you the curve of supply and demand, this illustration made it easier to understand the relationship between these two elements.

Using an Image in a Group

Using an image can be especially useful in a group setting, since a discussion will draw on the wisdom of the crowd to show the different ways in which people respond to the image. This will indicate the varied ways that a single image evokes multiple interpretations and meanings. In turn, people can come to recognize that there is no one correct way of viewing the image, because everyone sees and learns totally different things from the picture.

Using this image with a group is like showing everyone a map. Instead of it being a map that represents a series of roads, it is a map into the self, enabling self-discovery. It can also be a map into the imagination, in which the viewer creates his or her own roads and terrain. In this case, the map no longer represents an actual reality; rather it is used to create the reality that each person brings to the map, due to differences in backgrounds and experience, resulting in differently seeing the actual image.

This kind of seeing is a little bit like looking at the images in a Rorschach test, which is made up of a series of inkblots, which a person interprets. In the images below do you see a bug, a butterfly, two warriors fighting, a celebration, blood drippings from a wound, or what? Just as these images will be interpreted differently by different people, so will the cat and tiger and other images that people see.

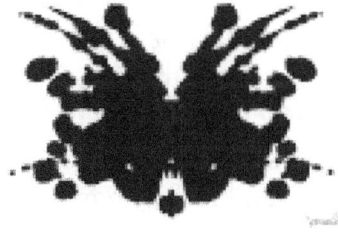

Even though other images may be realistic, unlike the abstract Rorschach images, they similarly evoke different responses from different people – and the initial responses can be like the opening into the cave of the mind. These then allow one to probe more deeply by oneself or with the help of a skilled counselor, coach, or other guide. Even a group of people in a workshop responding to these images can serve as a guide to help others in the group probe more deeply into themselves, as well as gain insights from the interpretations of others about what they see.

The Different Perceptions of the Same Picture

In using an image with a group, you can also point out that the perceptions people have in response to a particular image can change over time, depending on what people feel or need to learn for themselves at that moment. Or different people can have different perceptions in response to the same image.

While one woman saw the beauty in the tiger's eyes in the mirror, another woman saw sadness in the same eyes. What were the reasons for the differences? In the first case, the woman was excited about going on a vacation to an exotic location. She was already primed to think about beautiful things and came from a happy state of mind. By contrast, the other woman told the group that she had felt sad recently because she hadn't yet fulfilled her potential. She was already in a sad place in her life and seeing the images of the eyes triggered her feelings of sadness.

This approach can be used with other pictures, too. In this book I mainly refer to insights from the cat/tiger image, since it was especially empowering for me. I was drawn to it because of the way it shows a cat seeing itself as something bigger while it was looking in the mirror. Additionally, I found it is a perfect tool to encourage others to look in their own mirrors to find their true self, improve themselves, and discover their inner spark.

The More You Give the More You Get

Finally, you can point out to people in a group the importance of being kind, compassionate, and caring to others -- a principle I recognized after I heard a few people report seeing kindness in the tiger's eyes. While tigers may be very powerful, they also have the power to be kind.

As I explained at the workshop, some guides, teachers, and mentors will be soft and gentle when they know it is necessary to help others' growth. Moreover, being kind can help you seem even bigger to others, because you are helping them. Therefore, it is not surprising that we see the kindness in the eyes of tiger, which is the bigger cat, because kindness makes you bigger than life. Furthermore, the more you give, the more you get and the more you progress in life. When you are kind, even if you are little as a kitten, you feel bigger like a tiger.

This is an important message to share with the group you are training, because you are encouraging the attendees to have these qualities when they relate to others. You are also teaching them to impart this message, when they apply these principles in their own trainings of others.

* * *

Hopefully, you now have a deeper understanding of who you truly are and know to be positive, daring and caring. You also got a deep "see" into your soul and picture reading, and you see many more seas of possibilities.

In the future, when you look at the mirror and at the world in general, always look and see the bright side of yourself and your life. Find your inner spark and light the world with it. In this way you will:

SEE DEEP INTO YOUR SOUL AND FIND THE SEA OF POSSIBLITIES IN YOUR LIFE

I truly hope you enjoyed THE DEEP SEE. Since the possibilities for applying these principles are endless, and the goal is for everyone to grow, progress, and fulfill his or her potential, let's continue our conversation. Here are some ways you can do this, and I look forward to hearing from you:

Facebook: Naomi Bareket
Business Facebook: neuroSUCCESSology
www.neuroSUCCESSology.com
neuro@neurosuccessology.com

ABOUT THE AUTHOR

Naomi Bareket is the co-founder of NeuroSUCCESSology™. She leads Women Empowerment and Self-Fulfillment groups and seminar and workshops, using a combination of techniques. These include NLP (Neuro Linguistic Programming), hypnosis, Time Line Therapy®, neuro-science, Kabbalah, and others. Through these methods, she helps clients remove their fears, habits and other baggage holding them back from getting the results they seek. She helps people find their inner spark and personal motivators and identify any road blocks that stand in their way.

She developed these programs after wondering why she and others experienced fear, didn't feel fulfilled, or weren't living at full potential. After she discovered cutting edge tools and techniques to make her own breakthroughs, she saw the value in helping others live the lives they knew they deserved and created NeuroSUCCESSology™.

Naomi believes that the ultimate happiness occurs when you are in alignment with your life's true purpose and find your inner spark which lights up your soul. Then, you are empowered to give more and help others, too.

To help others find their true purpose and inner spark, Naomi has written *The Deep See* and other self-help and inspirational books, including *NeuroSUCCESSology™ -- Life Transformation,* and *The Jewish NLP.* Naomi additionally has a master's in business, is an expert in linguistics, and is an NLP trainer certified by the American Board, and she trains and certifies others at the practitioner and master levels.

www.ingramcontent.com/pod-product-compliance
Lightning Source LLC
LaVergne TN
LVHW021526080426
835509LV00018B/2676